Harvesting Prosperity: The Ultimate Guide to Homestead Income

Introduction: The Homesteading Advantage   7
   Introduction   7
   The Growing Popularity of Homesteading   7
   Potential for Income Generation   8
   Understanding the Unique Advantages   8
   Conclusion   10

Chapter 1: Assessing Your Resources and Setting Goals   13
   Introduction   13
   Evaluating Your Homestead's Assets   13
   Identifying Personal Goals and Financial Targets   14
      Tips and Tricks   15
   Conclusion   18

Chapter 2: Leveraging Sustainable Agriculture for Profit   21
   Introduction   21
   Selecting and Cultivating High-Value Crops Suited to Your Homestead   21
   Implementing Organic and Regenerative Farming Practices   22
   Exploring Niche Markets and Specialty Crops for Higher Profit Margins   23
   Conclusion   24
      Tips and Tricks: 25

Chapter 3: Exploring Alternative Energy Options on Your Homestead   29
   Introduction   29
   Harnessing Solar, Wind, or Hydro Power for Cost Savings and Potential Income   29
   Evaluating the Feasibility of Installing Renewable Energy Systems   30
   Conclusion   32

Tips and Tricks:	33
Chapter 4: Creating Value-Added Products from Your Harvest	**37**
Introduction	37
Understanding the Benefits of Value-Added Processing and Packaging	37
Techniques for Preserving, Canning, and Packaging Your Harvest	38
Developing a Product Line of Jams, Jellies, Pickles, Sauces, or Other Value-Added Items	39
Conclusion	40
Tips and Tricks:	41
Chapter 5: Tapping into the Agritourism Market	**45**
Introduction	45
Capitalizing on the Increasing Interest in Farm-to-Table Experiences and Agritourism	45
Creating Farm Tours, Workshops, or Educational Programs for Visitors	46
Exploring Opportunities for Farm Stays, On-Site Lodging, or Event Hosting	47
Conclusion	48
Chapter 6: Maximizing Your Livestock and Poultry Ventures	**53**
Introduction	53
Identifying Profitable Livestock and Poultry Breeds for Your Homestead	53
Strategies for Efficient Animal Husbandry, Feeding, and Healthcare	54
Expanding Income through Meat, Dairy, Eggs, or Fiber Production	55
Tips and Tricks:	57
Chapter 7: Harnessing the Power of Online Marketplaces	**60**
Introduction	60

    Establishing an Online Presence   60

    Optimizing Product Listings and Descriptions for SEO 61

    Leveraging Online Platforms for Wider Reach and Increased Sales   62

        Tips and Tricks: 64

Chapter 8: Diversifying Income Streams with Cottage Industries   67

    Introduction   67

    Exploring Additional Income Opportunities   67

    Developing Cottage Industries   68

    Balancing Diversification with Sustainability and Effective Time Management   69

        Tips and Tricks: 71

Chapter 9: Conclusion - Putting it all together for long-term success   74

    Introduction   74

    Summarizing the Key Strategies for Generating Income from Your Homestead   74

    Emphasizing the Importance of Ongoing Evaluation, Adaptation, and Growth   76

    Encouraging Readers to Pursue Their Homesteading Dreams and Achieve Financial Prosperity   77

From the Author   80

Worksheets   83

    Homestead Income Generation Checklist: 84

    Products you should consider selling on your homestead.   88

Appendix: Resources and Tools   90

Introduction: The Homesteading Advantage

Introduction

Homesteading has experienced a remarkable resurgence in recent years, with an increasing number of individuals and families embracing this lifestyle. Beyond the allure of self-sufficiency and a closer connection to nature, homesteading offers unique advantages for those seeking to generate income and achieve financial success. In this chapter, we explore the growing popularity of homesteading as a means of income generation and delve into the distinct advantages it offers in the pursuit of financial independence.

The Growing Popularity of Homesteading

In an era marked by rapid urbanization and a disconnection from the natural world, homesteading has captured the imaginations of many. People are drawn to the idea of returning to a simpler way of life, where they can have control over their food, reduce their environmental impact, and embrace a more sustainable lifestyle. The desire for self-sufficiency and a yearning to escape the stress of modern living have contributed to the increasing popularity of homesteading.

Potential for Income Generation

Homesteading offers a plethora of opportunities to generate income, making it an attractive option for those seeking financial independence. By leveraging the resources available on their land, homesteaders can tap into various income streams that align with their skills, interests, and local market demands. From sustainable agriculture and livestock production to value-added products and agritourism, the potential for income generation on a homestead is limited only by one's creativity and willingness to explore different avenues.

Understanding the Unique Advantages

Homesteading presents a range of unique advantages that set it apart from traditional employment or business ventures. These advantages contribute to the financial viability and sustainability of a homestead income:

- Low Overhead Costs: Homesteaders can significantly reduce their expenses by growing their own food, harnessing renewable energy sources, and embracing frugal living. With lower overhead costs, a higher portion of the income generated can be retained, leading to increased profitability.

- Increased Self-Sufficiency: Homesteading fosters self-reliance by producing one's food, generating energy, and managing resources sustainably. This self-sufficiency not only reduces reliance on external systems but also positions homesteaders to capitalize on rising consumer demand for locally sourced, organic, and sustainable products.

- Diversification and Resilience: Homesteaders can diversify their income streams by pursuing multiple ventures simultaneously. This diversification not only spreads risk but also ensures a more resilient and stable financial foundation, as different income sources may have varying performance levels.

- Lifestyle Integration: Homesteading allows individuals to integrate their lifestyle preferences with their income-generating activities. It enables individuals to work from home, spend more time with family, and align their values with their livelihood. This integration fosters a sense of fulfillment and purpose, which can positively impact both personal and financial well-being.

Conclusion

Homesteading offers a unique pathway to financial success, combining the benefits of self-sufficiency, low overhead costs, diversification, and a more integrated and fulfilling lifestyle. As the popularity of homesteading continues to grow, more individuals are recognizing the potential for generating income while embracing a simpler, more sustainable way of life. By understanding and leveraging the advantages of homesteading, you can embark on a journey towards financial independence and prosperity, all while living harmoniously with the land.

Chapter 1: Assessing Your Resources and Setting Goals

Introduction

Before embarking on your journey to generate income from your homestead, it is essential to assess the resources available to you and establish clear goals. This chapter serves as a comprehensive guide to evaluating your homestead's assets, including land, climate, and infrastructure, and helps you identify your personal goals and financial targets for homestead income.

Evaluating Your Homestead's Assets

Land: Begin by assessing the size, topography, and quality of your land. Consider its suitability for various agricultural activities, such as crop cultivation, livestock grazing, or orchard establishment. Determine any limitations, such as soil fertility, water availability, or zoning restrictions that may impact your income-generating potential.

Climate: Understand the climate patterns specific to your region. Evaluate factors like average temperatures, precipitation levels, frost dates, and growing seasons. This information will guide you in selecting crops, livestock breeds, or alternative energy sources that align with the climatic conditions of your homestead.

Infrastructure: Take stock of the existing infrastructure on your homestead, including buildings, fences, irrigation systems, and equipment. Assess their condition, functionality, and capacity to support your income-generating activities. Determine any necessary repairs, upgrades, or additional investments needed to maximize efficiency and productivity.

Identifying Personal Goals and Financial Targets

Reflect on Your Passions and Interests: Consider the activities that bring you joy and fulfillment. Identify areas where you have knowledge or skills that can be applied to your homestead income endeavors. Aligning your goals with your passions will increase your motivation and overall satisfaction.

Define Your Financial Targets: Determine the level of income you aim to generate from your homestead. Set specific, measurable, achievable, relevant, and time-bound (SMART) financial targets that reflect your personal and financial aspirations. Consider both short-term and long-term goals to ensure a balanced approach.

Prioritize and Select Income Streams: Explore the various income-generating opportunities available on a homestead, such as sustainable agriculture, livestock production, value-added products, agritourism, or online sales. Prioritize the options that align with your resources, interests, and financial targets.

Tips and Tricks

- Seek Expert Advice: Consult with local agricultural extension offices, experienced homesteaders, or professionals in relevant fields. Their expertise can provide valuable insights into maximizing your homestead's income potential.

- Conduct Market Research: Understand the local and regional market demand for your potential products or services. Identify gaps, niche markets, or unique selling propositions that can give you a competitive advantage.

- Start Small and Scale Up: Begin with manageable projects and gradually expand as you gain experience and confidence. This approach minimizes risk while allowing you to learn and adapt along the way.

- Embrace Continuous Learning: Stay informed about the latest advancements, best practices, and market trends in your chosen income streams. Attend workshops, conferences, or join online communities to connect with fellow homesteaders and industry experts.

- Track and Evaluate Performance: Establish a system for monitoring and evaluating the performance of your income-generating activities. Regularly assess profitability, resource utilization, and customer satisfaction to make informed decisions and adjustments.

- Engage in soil testing to determine soil composition and nutrient levels, enabling you to make informed decisions about crop rotation, fertilization, and soil amendment.

- Consider diversifying your income streams to minimize risk and take advantage of multiple revenue sources.

- Utilize online resources and platforms to research market trends, connect with potential customers, and promote your homestead products or services.

- Network with other homesteaders and agricultural professionals to learn from their experiences and gain valuable insights.

- Keep detailed records of your expenses, sales, and profits to track the financial performance of your income-generating activities.

- Stay adaptable and open to exploring new opportunities and adjusting your strategies as needed to meet evolving market demands.

- Prioritize sustainable and environmentally friendly practices in your income-generating activities to appeal to eco-conscious consumers.

- Consider the potential for value-added products or unique offerings that set your homestead apart from competitors.

- Continuously invest in your own education and skills development to enhance your expertise and stay ahead in the industry.

By following these tips and tricks, you can make informed decisions, optimize your homestead's resources, and set achievable goals for your income-generating ventures.

Conclusion

Assessing your homestead's resources and setting clear goals is a critical foundation for achieving financial success. By evaluating your land, climate, infrastructure, and aligning your personal aspirations with specific financial targets, you lay the groundwork for selecting the most suitable income streams for your homestead. Remember to seek expert advice, conduct market research, start small, and embrace continuous learning to enhance your chances of success.

Chapter 2: Leveraging Sustainable Agriculture for Profit

Introduction

Sustainable agriculture forms the cornerstone of many successful homestead income strategies. By selecting and cultivating high-value crops, implementing organic and regenerative farming practices, and exploring niche markets and specialty crops, homesteaders can maximize their yields and profitability. This chapter delves into the strategies and techniques necessary to leverage sustainable agriculture for financial success on your homestead.

Selecting and Cultivating High-Value Crops Suited to Your Homestead

Assessing Market Demand: Research local and regional market demand to identify high-value crops that are in demand and have the potential for higher profit margins. Consider factors such as consumer preferences, emerging trends, and the suitability of your homestead's resources for growing specific crops.

Evaluating Environmental Factors: Analyze the climate, soil conditions, and available water resources on your homestead to determine which crops are best suited for your location. Consider the growing season, temperature tolerance, water requirements, and disease resistance of different crops to make informed choices.

Diversification and Crop Rotation: Embrace diversification by cultivating a variety of crops. This not only spreads risk but also allows you to take advantage of different market seasons and consumer preferences. Implementing crop rotation practices helps improve soil health, reduce pest and disease pressure, and enhance overall yields.

Implementing Organic and Regenerative Farming Practices

Organic Certification: Explore the process of obtaining organic certification for your crops. Adhering to organic farming practices can open doors to premium markets, commanding higher prices for your produce. Learn about organic standards, prohibited substances, and record-keeping requirements to ensure compliance.

Soil Health and Fertility: Prioritize soil health by implementing practices such as cover cropping, composting, and the use of organic amendments. These practices enhance soil fertility, promote beneficial microbial activity, and improve nutrient availability to plants, resulting in higher yields and better-quality produce.

Integrated Pest Management (IPM): Implement an IPM approach that focuses on preventive measures, biological controls, and minimal use of pesticides. By promoting natural predators, using crop rotation, practicing proper sanitation, and monitoring pest populations, you can effectively manage pests while reducing reliance on synthetic chemical inputs.

Exploring Niche Markets and Specialty Crops for Higher Profit Margins

Researching Niche Markets: Identify niche markets that align with your homestead's unique offerings, such as heirloom varieties, ethnic or gourmet crops, or medicinal herbs. Research consumer preferences, attend local farmers' markets, and engage with potential buyers to understand market demand and develop a niche marketing strategy.

Specialty Crop Production: Consider growing specialty crops that command higher prices due to their unique qualities or limited availability. Examples include heirloom tomatoes, specialty herbs, microgreens, or rare varieties of fruits and vegetables. Research cultivation techniques, post-harvest handling, and marketing strategies specific to these specialty crops.

Value-Added Products: Explore the potential for value-added products derived from your crops, such as jams, sauces, herbal teas, or dried herbs. Value-added products not only increase profit margins but also extend the shelf life of your produce and provide opportunities for branding and marketing your homestead's unique offerings.

Conclusion

Leveraging sustainable agriculture is a powerful way to generate income on your homestead. By carefully selecting high-value crops suited to your homestead, implementing organic and regenerative farming practices, and exploring niche markets and specialty crops, you can increase yields, command higher prices, and tap into unique opportunities. Embrace the principles of sustainability, market research, and innovation to maximize profitability and pave the way for a thriving and financially rewarding homestead income.

Tips and Tricks:

1. Stay informed about emerging market trends and consumer preferences to identify new opportunities and adapt your farming practices accordingly.

2. Network with local chefs, restaurants, and specialty food stores to establish direct sales channels for your high-value crops and value-added products.

3. Consider participating in farmers' markets, community-supported agriculture (CSA) programs, or farm-to-table initiatives to connect directly with consumers and build a loyal customer base.

4. Utilize social media and online platforms to showcase your sustainable farming practices, unique crops, and value-added products, reaching a wider audience and attracting potential customers.

5. Collaborate with other local farmers or homesteaders to pool resources, share knowledge, and collectively market your products, increasing your visibility and competitiveness.

6. Continuously educate yourself on sustainable farming techniques, organic certification processes, and niche market trends through workshops, online courses, and industry publications.

7. Keep detailed records of crop yields, expenses, and market performance to evaluate the profitability of different crops and inform future decision-making.

8. Prioritize building strong relationships with your customers by providing exceptional product quality, personalized customer service, and engaging storytelling about your sustainable farming practices.

9. Regularly review and reassess your crop selection, farming practices, and marketing strategies to adapt to changing market conditions and maximize profitability.

10. Embrace a mindset of continuous improvement, seeking ways to enhance your farming methods,

expand your product offerings, and differentiate yourself in the marketplace.

By incorporating these tips and tricks into your sustainable agriculture practices, you can position your homestead for success in generating income through high-value crops, organic farming, and niche market exploration. Remember that sustainable agriculture is not only economically rewarding but also contributes to the health of your land, the well-being of your community, and the preservation of our environment.

Chapter 3: Exploring Alternative Energy Options on Your Homestead

Introduction

In today's world, harnessing alternative energy sources on your homestead not only provides cost savings but also offers the potential for income generation. This chapter explores the various alternative energy options available, such as solar, wind, or hydro power, and provides guidance on evaluating the feasibility of installing renewable energy systems on your homestead. Additionally, it discusses government incentives and grants that can support your renewable energy projects.

Harnessing Solar, Wind, or Hydro Power for Cost Savings and Potential Income

Solar Power: Understand the benefits of solar energy and how it can be harnessed on your homestead.

Explore the different types of solar systems, including photovoltaic (PV) panels and solar water heaters. Assess your energy needs and determine the appropriate size and capacity of the solar system required to meet your homestead's requirements.

Wind Power: Evaluate the potential of wind energy by considering factors such as average wind speeds, local regulations, and the suitability of your land for wind turbine installation. Determine the energy needs that can be met through wind power and assess the feasibility and financial viability of integrating wind turbines into your homestead's energy infrastructure.

Hydro Power: If you have a water source such as a stream or river on your homestead, explore the possibility of harnessing hydro power. Assess the water flow, elevation change, and potential power generation capacity. Consider micro-hydro systems that can provide a sustainable and reliable source of energy for your homestead.

Evaluating the Feasibility of Installing Renewable Energy Systems

Energy Audit: Conduct an energy audit to assess your current energy consumption patterns and identify areas of improvement. This evaluation will help you determine the appropriate scale and type of renewable energy system needed to meet your homestead's energy demands.

Site Assessment: Evaluate your homestead's location, available space, and natural resources to determine the suitability for renewable energy installations. Consider factors such as shading, wind patterns, water flow, and terrain characteristics. Assess potential constraints and opportunities for optimal energy production.

Financial Analysis: Perform a comprehensive financial analysis to evaluate the return on investment (ROI) of installing renewable energy systems. Consider the initial installation costs, ongoing maintenance expenses, potential energy savings, and income generation opportunities. Calculate payback periods and assess long-term financial benefits.

Exploring Government Incentives and Grants for Renewable Energy Projects

Research Government Programs: Explore local, state, and federal government programs that provide incentives, grants, or tax credits for renewable energy projects. Familiarize yourself with eligibility criteria, application processes, and available funding options. Examples may include the USDA Rural Energy for America Program (REAP) or state-level clean energy initiatives.

Engage with Energy Agencies and Organizations: Connect with energy agencies, environmental organizations, or industry associations that provide guidance and support for renewable energy projects. These entities can provide valuable information on available incentives, technical assistance, and networking opportunities within the renewable energy sector.

Consult with Experts: Seek professional advice from renewable energy experts, engineers, or contractors who specialize in designing and installing renewable energy systems. They can help assess the feasibility of your project, provide cost estimates, and guide you through the application process for government incentives or grants.

Conclusion

Exploring alternative energy options on your homestead offers significant benefits, including cost savings, energy independence, and potential income generation. By harnessing solar, wind, or hydro power, you can reduce your reliance on conventional energy sources and contribute to a more sustainable future. Evaluate the feasibility of renewable energy systems on your homestead, considering factors such as energy needs, site suitability, and financial analysis. Additionally, take advantage of government incentives and grants that can provide crucial support for your renewable energy projects.

Tips and Tricks:

Conduct a thorough analysis of your energy needs to determine the appropriate size and capacity of the renewable energy system. Consider factors such as electricity consumption, heating and cooling requirements, and any potential future expansions.

Research reputable suppliers and installers of renewable energy systems. Request quotes, compare prices, and review customer testimonials to ensure you choose a reliable and experienced provider.

Regularly maintain and monitor your renewable energy systems to ensure optimal performance and longevity. This includes cleaning solar panels, inspecting wind turbine components, and maintaining proper water flow for hydro systems.

Explore energy storage options such as batteries or pumped hydro storage to store excess energy generated by your renewable systems. This allows you to utilize the energy during low-production periods or sell it back to the grid, further increasing your income potential.

Educate yourself about net metering policies and regulations in your area. Net metering allows you to receive credits or monetary compensation for excess energy fed back into the grid.

Consider integrating energy-efficient practices and appliances into your homestead. This will help maximize the efficiency of your renewable energy systems and further reduce your overall energy consumption.

Engage with your local community and share your experience with renewable energy. By promoting the benefits and advantages of clean energy, you can inspire others to consider similar initiatives, potentially leading to a more sustainable community as a whole.

Continuously stay updated on technological advancements and industry trends in renewable energy. New innovations and improvements may present opportunities to optimize your existing systems or explore additional renewable energy options on your homestead.

By following these tips and tricks, you can confidently explore and implement alternative energy options on your homestead. Harnessing solar, wind, or hydro power not only provides cost savings but also positions your homestead as a sustainable and environmentally conscious enterprise. Furthermore, taking advantage of government incentives and grants can significantly support your renewable energy projects and enhance the financial viability of your homestead income.

Chapter 4: Creating Value-Added Products from Your Harvest

Introduction

Transforming your homestead harvest into value-added products offers numerous benefits, including extended shelf life, higher prices, and the opportunity to tap into niche markets. This chapter explores the concept of value-added processing and packaging, providing insights into the advantages it brings. It also delves into techniques for preserving, canning, and packaging your harvest, as well as guidance on developing a product line of jams, jellies, pickles, sauces, or other value-added items.

Understanding the Benefits of Value-Added Processing and Packaging

Extended Shelf Life: Value-added processing techniques such as canning, preserving, and packaging can significantly extend the shelf life of your homestead harvest. This allows you to store and sell your products throughout the year, reducing waste and increasing revenue potential.

Higher Prices: By transforming your raw produce into value-added products, you can command higher prices compared to selling fresh produce alone. Consumers are often willing to pay a premium for unique flavors, artisanal quality, and locally made goods.

Market Differentiation: Value-added products provide an opportunity to differentiate your homestead's offerings from competitors. By developing a distinct product line, you can attract customers seeking specialty items and niche market segments.

Techniques for Preserving, Canning, and Packaging Your Harvest

Canning: Learn the art of canning, which involves preserving fruits, vegetables, and other foods in jars through heat processing. Explore both water bath canning and pressure canning methods, depending on the type of produce you wish to preserve. Understand the proper procedures for sterilization, filling jars, and achieving airtight seals to ensure product safety and longevity.

Freezing: Freezing is a simple and effective method for preserving fruits, vegetables, and herbs. Properly blanch and cool the produce before freezing to maintain quality. Invest in quality freezer storage containers or vacuum-sealing equipment to prevent freezer burn and maintain the flavor and texture of your harvest.

Drying: Drying is a traditional method of preserving fruits, vegetables, herbs, and even meat. Explore various drying techniques, such as sun drying, air drying, or using dehydrators. Properly dry your produce to remove moisture and prevent spoilage. Store the dried items in airtight containers to maintain their quality and flavor.

Developing a Product Line of Jams, Jellies, Pickles, Sauces, or Other Value-Added Items

Recipe Development: Experiment with recipes and flavors to create unique and delicious value-added products. Consider the preferences and tastes of your target market while incorporating your homestead's signature ingredients or flavors. Test and refine your recipes to ensure consistent quality and taste.

Packaging and Labeling: Invest in attractive packaging materials that showcase the quality and appeal of your value-added products. Develop eye-catching labels that comply with food labeling regulations and clearly communicate product information, ingredients, and any certifications or special features.

Branding and Marketing: Create a compelling brand identity for your value-added product line. Develop a brand story that highlights your homestead's values, sustainability practices, and local sourcing. Utilize various marketing channels, including social media, farmers' markets, online platforms, and local stores, to promote and sell your products.

Conclusion

Creating value-added products from your homestead harvest opens up new avenues for income generation and market differentiation. By understanding the benefits of value-added processing and packaging, mastering preservation techniques, and developing a unique product line, you can extend the shelf life of your harvest, command higher prices, and cater to niche market segments. Embrace the art of canning, freezing, and drying while exploring recipes, packaging, and branding strategies to successfully create and market your value added products. Here are some additional tips and tricks to enhance your success in creating value-added products:

Tips and Tricks:

Conduct Market Research: Prior to developing your product line, research the market demand for value-added products in your area. Identify potential competitors, understand consumer preferences, and seek out untapped market niches. This information will help you tailor your offerings to meet market needs effectively.

Consider Seasonality: Take advantage of seasonal produce availability when developing your value-added product line. This allows you to maximize the use of fresh ingredients and create a sense of anticipation among customers for limited-time offerings.

Quality Control: Maintain high standards of quality control throughout the value-added processing and packaging process. Implement strict hygiene practices, use fresh and top-quality ingredients, and regularly inspect your products for any signs of spoilage or deterioration.

Develop Relationships with Suppliers: Cultivate strong relationships with local farmers, growers, or other suppliers to ensure a consistent and reliable source of high-quality ingredients. Collaborating with local producers can also help foster a sense of community and support the local economy.

Experiment with Flavor Combinations: Push the boundaries of flavor by experimenting with unique and innovative combinations of ingredients. Consider incorporating herbs, spices, or other locally sourced elements to create distinctive and memorable flavors that set your products apart.

Seek Customer Feedback: Engage with your customers to gather feedback on your value-added products. Consider hosting tasting events, conducting surveys, or actively soliciting feedback through online platforms. Use this valuable input to refine your products and cater to evolving customer preferences.

Develop Distribution Channels: Explore various distribution channels to reach your target market effectively. This can include partnering with local stores, participating in farmers' markets, establishing an online presence, or even considering wholesale options. Diversifying your distribution channels expands your customer reach and increases the visibility of your products.

Emphasize Sustainable Packaging: Consider environmentally friendly packaging options that align with your homestead's sustainability values. Choose materials that are recyclable, reusable, or biodegradable whenever possible. This demonstrates your commitment to sustainable practices and resonates with eco-conscious consumers.

Continuously Innovate: Keep abreast of market trends, emerging flavors, and evolving consumer preferences. Regularly innovate and introduce new value-added products to keep your offerings fresh and exciting. This ensures that your product line remains competitive and captivating to your target audience.

Build a Strong Brand Reputation: Focus on building a strong brand reputation based on consistent quality, excellent customer service, and transparent business practices. Positive word-of-mouth recommendations and customer loyalty will contribute significantly to the long-term success of your value-added products.

By incorporating these tips and tricks, you can effectively create, market, and sell value-added products from your homestead harvest. The ability to transform your raw produce into unique, shelf-stable items not only increases your revenue potential but also allows you to showcase the flavors and essence of your homestead, resonating with customers who appreciate locally made, artisanal goods.

Chapter 5: Tapping into the Agritourism Market

Introduction

The agritourism market presents a lucrative opportunity for homesteaders to capitalize on the growing interest in farm-to-table experiences and sustainable living. This chapter explores the benefits of tapping into the agritourism market and provides insights into creating farm tours, workshops, or educational programs for visitors. It also delves into opportunities for offering farm stays, on-site lodging, or hosting events, allowing you to generate additional income while showcasing the unique aspects of your homestead.

Capitalizing on the Increasing Interest in Farm-to-Table Experiences and Agritourism

Market Demand: Agritourism is gaining popularity as consumers seek authentic, educational, and immersive experiences that connect them to the source of their food. The demand for farm-to-table experiences, agricultural education, and sustainable living practices provides an ideal opportunity for homesteaders to tap into the agritourism market.

Diversified Income: Engaging in agritourism allows you to diversify your income streams beyond traditional farming or selling produce alone. By offering unique experiences and services, you can generate additional revenue and enhance the overall financial sustainability of your homestead.

Creating Farm Tours, Workshops, or Educational Programs for Visitors

Farm Tours: Develop engaging and informative farm tours that showcase the various aspects of your homestead. Highlight sustainable farming practices, animal husbandry, crop cultivation, and any other unique features. Provide visitors with hands-on experiences and opportunities to connect with nature and farm life.

Workshops and Classes: Offer workshops or classes on topics such as organic gardening, composting, food preservation, or sustainable living practices. Share your knowledge and expertise with participants, empowering them to adopt similar practices in their own lives. Consider partnering with local experts or organizations to enhance the value and diversity of your educational offerings.

Children's Programs: Develop educational programs specifically tailored for children, such as farm-themed day camps or field trips. Incorporate interactive activities, animal interactions, and hands-on learning experiences to engage and educate young visitors about agriculture and sustainability.

Exploring Opportunities for Farm Stays, On-Site Lodging, or Event Hosting

Farm Stays: Capitalize on the rising popularity of farm stays by offering on-site lodging accommodations for visitors. Create a comfortable and welcoming environment where guests can experience rural living, participate in farm activities, and enjoy the tranquility of your homestead. Provide unique amenities and services that showcase the charm and authenticity of your farm.

Event Hosting: Utilize your homestead's natural beauty and rustic charm to host events such as weddings, corporate retreats, or agricultural fairs. Develop partnerships with event planners, caterers, and other service providers to offer comprehensive event packages. Ensure that your facilities can accommodate different types of events and have the necessary amenities and infrastructure.

Farm-to-Table Experiences: Organize farm-to-table dining experiences, where visitors can enjoy meals prepared using fresh produce from your homestead. Collaborate with local chefs or culinary experts to create unique and memorable dining experiences that highlight the flavors and quality of your farm's harvest.

Conclusion

Tapping into the agritourism market provides homesteaders with a remarkable opportunity to share their farming practices, educate visitors, and generate additional income. By capitalizing on the increasing interest in farm-to-table experiences and sustainable living, you can create farm tours, workshops, or educational programs that cater to diverse audiences. Furthermore, exploring opportunities for farm stays, on-site lodging, or event hosting allows you to provide immersive and unforgettable experiences for visitors while enhancing the financial sustainability of your homestead. Embrace the agritourism market and leverage the unique aspects of your farm to offer engaging and enriching experiences that connect people with the land, food production, and sustainable living practices.

Tips and Tricks:

Here are some additional tips and tricks to enhance your success in tapping into the agritourism market:

Know Your Target Audience: Understand the preferences, interests, and demographics of your target audience. Tailor your agritourism offerings to cater to their specific needs, whether it's families with children, food enthusiasts, nature lovers, or those seeking educational experiences.

Create Memorable Experiences: Focus on providing unique and memorable experiences that set your homestead apart. Incorporate interactive elements, hands-on activities, and opportunities for visitors to connect with animals, crops, and the natural environment. Aim to create lasting impressions that visitors will cherish and share with others.

Collaborate with Local Partners: Forge partnerships with local businesses, tourism boards, and community organizations to amplify your agritourism offerings. Collaborate on joint marketing initiatives, cross-promote each other's services, and tap into their networks to attract a wider audience.

Offer Customizable Packages: Provide customizable agritourism packages that cater to different interests and group sizes. Allow visitors to choose from a range of activities, duration of stay, or combination of workshops and farm experiences. This flexibility ensures that you can accommodate a diverse range of visitors and their preferences.

Prioritize Safety and Liability: Ensure that your agritourism activities comply with all safety regulations and carry the necessary insurance coverage. Implement appropriate safety measures, provide clear instructions to visitors, and regularly inspect your facilities and equipment to minimize the risk of accidents.

Implement Sustainable Practices: Emphasize your homestead's commitment to sustainability by implementing eco-friendly practices in your agritourism operations. Use renewable energy, promote recycling and waste reduction, practice responsible water usage, and source locally produced materials whenever possible. This demonstrates your dedication to environmental stewardship, which resonates with sustainability-minded visitors.

Engage with Social Media: Utilize social media platforms to showcase your agritourism offerings, share behind-the-scenes glimpses of farm life, and interact with potential visitors. Use visually appealing content, storytelling, and user-generated content to create an authentic and engaging online presence. Encourage visitors to share their experiences and reviews to generate positive word-of-mouth.

Collect Visitor Feedback: Regularly seek feedback from your agritourism visitors to understand their experiences and identify areas for improvement. Provide comment cards, online surveys, or feedback forms to gather valuable insights that can help you refine and enhance your offerings over time.

Stay Educated and Evolve: Continuously educate yourself about agritourism trends, best practices, and emerging opportunities. Attend workshops, conferences, and industry events to network with other agritourism professionals and stay up-to-date with the latest developments in the field. Adapt your offerings to changing consumer preferences and market demands.

By incorporating these tips and tricks into your agritourism strategy, you can create a unique and successful experience for visitors while leveraging the natural beauty and resources of your homestead. Embrace the agritourism market as a means to not only generate additional income but also to educate, inspire, and foster connections between people and the land.

Chapter 6: Maximizing Your Livestock and Poultry Ventures

Introduction

Maximizing the potential of your livestock and poultry ventures can significantly contribute to the financial success of your homestead. This chapter explores various strategies to help you identify profitable livestock and poultry breeds, implement efficient animal husbandry practices, and expand your income through meat, dairy, eggs, or fiber production. By optimizing your livestock and poultry operations, you can increase profitability and enhance the sustainability of your homestead.

Identifying Profitable Livestock and Poultry Breeds for Your Homestead

Assessing Market Demand: Research and analyze the local market demand for different livestock and poultry products. Consider factors such as consumer preferences, niche markets, and potential competition.

Identify breeds that have high demand and are well-suited to your homestead's resources, climate, and target market.

Evaluating Profitability: Assess the profitability of different livestock and poultry breeds by considering factors such as feed conversion rates, growth rates, market prices, and production costs. Consult with experienced breeders, agricultural extension offices, or local farming networks to gather insights and data on breed performance and market trends.

Diversification: Consider diversifying your livestock and poultry portfolio to maximize income potential. Explore raising multiple breeds or species that complement each other in terms of market cycles, production inputs, and consumer preferences. Diversification can help mitigate risks and provide a steady income stream throughout the year.

Strategies for Efficient Animal Husbandry, Feeding, and Healthcare

Housing and Infrastructure: Provide adequate housing and infrastructure that meets the specific needs of your livestock and poultry. Ensure proper ventilation, temperature control, and access to clean water and nutritious feed. Design your facilities to promote animal health, reduce stress, and facilitate efficient management practices.

Nutrition and Feeding: Develop a comprehensive feeding program tailored to the nutritional requirements of your livestock and poultry. Utilize a combination of pasture grazing, forage production, and balanced supplemental feed to optimize growth, reproduction, and overall health. Consult with a nutritionist or veterinarian to formulate appropriate diets for different life stages and production goals.

Animal Health and Disease Prevention: Implement proactive health management practices to prevent the occurrence and spread of diseases. Develop a vaccination schedule, practice biosecurity measures, and conduct regular health checks. Establish a relationship with a veterinarian who specializes in livestock and poultry to ensure proper care, diagnosis, and treatment when necessary.

Expanding Income through Meat, Dairy, Eggs, or Fiber Production

Meat Production: Explore opportunities to market and sell meat products from your livestock, such as beef, pork, lamb, or poultry. Consider direct-to-consumer sales, partnerships with local butcher shops or restaurants, or participation in farmers' markets. Emphasize the quality, traceability, and sustainable production practices of your meat products to attract discerning customers.

Dairy Production: If suitable for your homestead, consider incorporating dairy animals like cows, goats, or sheep for milk production. Process the milk into cheese, yogurt, butter, or other value-added dairy products. Establish distribution channels, such as local grocery stores, farmers' markets, or farm-to-door delivery services, to reach consumers interested in fresh and locally sourced dairy products.

Egg Production: Capitalize on the demand for fresh, organic, and free-range eggs by raising laying hens. Market your eggs as high-quality, nutrient-dense, and ethically produced. Consider selling directly to consumers, restaurants, health food stores, or participating in community-supported agriculture (CSA) programs.

Fiber Production: If you have fiber-producing animals like sheep, alpacas, or rabbits, explore the potential of fiber production for textiles, yarn, or crafts. Establish connections with local artisans, fiber enthusiasts, or fiber cooperatives to market and sell your fiber products. Participate in fiber festivals, craft fairs, or online platforms dedicated to handmade and locally sourced goods.

Tips and Tricks:

Research Breeds: Conduct thorough research on different livestock and poultry breeds to identify those that align with your homestead's resources and market demands. Consider factors such as adaptability to your climate, disease resistance, productivity, and consumer preferences.

Seek Expert Advice: Connect with experienced breeders, livestock extension agents, or agricultural professionals to gain valuable insights and guidance. Their expertise can help you make informed decisions regarding breed selection, animal management, and market trends.

Start Small and Scale Up: If you're new to livestock or poultry ventures, consider starting with a small number of animals to gain experience and confidence. As you become more proficient and knowledgeable, gradually expand your operations while ensuring you can manage the increased workload effectively.

Continual Education: Stay updated on advancements in animal husbandry practices, nutrition, and healthcare. Attend workshops, conferences, or webinars to learn from experts and stay informed about industry trends and best practices.

Networking and Collaboration: Join local farming organizations, livestock breed associations, or online communities to network with fellow farmers. Sharing experiences, knowledge, and resources can be mutually beneficial and open up opportunities for collaboration or joint marketing efforts.

Value-Added Products: Consider adding value to your livestock and poultry products by offering specialty or niche items. For example, create unique meat cuts, gourmet cheese blends, flavored eggs, or naturally dyed fibers. Differentiating your products can attract niche markets and command higher prices.

Direct Marketing: Explore direct marketing channels such as farm stands, CSA programs, online platforms, or farm-to-table restaurants. Direct marketing allows you to establish a personal connection with customers and communicate the unique qualities of your products.

Build Customer Relationships: Foster strong relationships with your customers by providing exceptional product quality, customer service, and transparency. Engage with them through social media, newsletters, or farm events to keep them informed and involved in your livestock and poultry ventures.

Value Sustainability: Emphasize your commitment to sustainable farming practices, animal welfare, and environmental stewardship. Highlight your efforts to consumers, as there is a growing demand for ethically and sustainably produced livestock and poultry products.

By implementing these strategies and following the tips and tricks outlined in this chapter, you can maximize the potential of your livestock and poultry ventures. Efficient animal husbandry practices, careful breed selection, and diversification of products can help you increase profitability and meet the demands of the market while maintaining the health and well-being of your animals.

Chapter 7: Harnessing the Power of Online Marketplaces

Introduction

In today's digital age, harnessing the power of online marketplaces is crucial for expanding your reach, increasing sales, and maximizing the profitability of your homestead. This chapter explores strategies to establish a strong online presence through websites, social media, and online marketplaces. You will learn how to optimize product listings and descriptions for search engine optimization (SEO) and leverage online platforms to reach a wider audience and drive sales.

Establishing an Online Presence

Build a Professional Website: Create a professional website that showcases your homestead, products, and brand. Invest in a user-friendly design that reflects the essence of your business. Include essential information such as contact details, product listings, pricing, and shipping information. Ensure that your website is responsive and compatible with mobile devices for a seamless user experience.

Engage on Social Media: Leverage popular social media platforms such as Facebook, Instagram, Twitter, or Pinterest to engage with your audience and promote your homestead. Share compelling visual content, stories, updates, and behind-the-scenes glimpses of your operations. Encourage interaction and respond to comments and inquiries promptly.

Utilize Online Marketplaces: Expand your online presence by listing your products on established online marketplaces like Etsy, Amazon, eBay, or local agricultural platforms. Research and select platforms that align with your target market and product offerings. Utilize the built-in customer base, marketing tools, and logistics support offered by these platforms to streamline your operations.

Optimizing Product Listings and Descriptions for SEO

Keyword Research: Conduct thorough keyword research to identify relevant and high-ranking keywords related to your products and homestead. Use tools like Google Keyword Planner or other SEO software to discover keywords with high search volume and low competition. Incorporate these keywords naturally into your product listings and descriptions.

Compelling Product Descriptions: Write engaging and informative product descriptions that highlight the unique features, benefits, and story behind your products. Use persuasive language, storytelling techniques, and compelling visuals to capture the attention of potential customers and differentiate your products from competitors.

High-Quality Visuals: Invest in high-quality product photography that showcases your products in the best light. Use professional-grade equipment or hire a photographer if necessary. Ensure that your images accurately represent the size, color, texture, and details of your products.

Leveraging Online Platforms for Wider Reach and Increased Sales

Online Advertising: Utilize online advertising platforms like Google Ads, Facebook Ads, or Instagram Ads to reach a wider audience and drive targeted traffic to your online platforms. Develop strategic ad campaigns that align with your target market, budget, and specific objectives.

Collaborate with Influencers: Identify influencers or bloggers in your niche who align with your brand values and target audience. Collaborate with them to promote your products through sponsored content, product reviews, or giveaways. Influencer marketing can help you tap into their loyal following and expand your reach.

Customer Reviews and Testimonials: Encourage satisfied customers to leave reviews and testimonials on your website, social media, or online marketplace listings. Positive reviews and ratings not only build trust and credibility but also improve your visibility in search results.

Customer Engagement and Support: Prioritize customer engagement and support by promptly responding to inquiries, providing accurate and detailed product information, and delivering excellent customer service. Engage with your customers through comments, direct messages, or email newsletters to foster long-term relationships and repeat business.

Analyze Data and Optimize: Regularly analyze data from your website, social media, and online marketplace platforms. Utilize analytics tools to gain insights into customer behavior, sales patterns, and marketing performance. Optimize your strategies based on the data to improve conversion rates, customer retention and overall online performance.

Tips and Tricks:

Consistent Branding: Maintain a consistent branding across all your online platforms, including your website, social media profiles, and online marketplace listings. Use consistent logos, colors, fonts, and messaging to create a cohesive and recognizable brand identity.

Professional Product Photography: Invest in high-quality product photography that accurately showcases the features and details of your products. Clear, well-lit images can significantly impact customer perception and increase the likelihood of making a sale.

Engage with the Online Community: Participate in online forums, groups, or communities related to your homesteading niche. Engage in conversations, answer questions, and share your knowledge and expertise. Building relationships within the online community can generate interest in your products and attract potential customers.

Offer Special Promotions: Run occasional promotions, discounts, or limited-time offers to create a sense of urgency and incentivize purchases. Promote these offers through your website, social media, and online marketplace listings to attract new customers and encourage repeat business.

Customer Testimonials and Social Proof: Highlight positive customer testimonials and social proof on your website and online marketplace listings. This builds trust and confidence in potential customers and increases the likelihood of making a purchase.

Monitor and Respond to Customer Feedback: Regularly monitor customer reviews, feedback, and comments across your online platforms. Respond promptly and professionally to both positive and negative feedback, showing that you value customer satisfaction and are committed to continuous improvement.

Collaborate with Complementary Businesses: Seek opportunities to collaborate with complementary businesses in your local area or within your niche. This could include cross-promotions, joint marketing campaigns, or even bundling products together to create attractive packages.

Stay Updated on Online Trends: Stay informed about emerging trends, changes in online algorithms, and new features or tools offered by online platforms. Keeping up with industry news and updates allows you to adapt your online marketing strategies and take advantage of new opportunities.

By harnessing the power of online marketplaces, optimizing your product listings for SEO, and leveraging social media platforms, you can significantly expand your reach and increase sales for your homestead products. Stay proactive, engage with your online community, and continually optimize your online presence to stay competitive in the digital marketplace.

Chapter 8: Diversifying Income Streams with Cottage Industries

Introduction

Diversifying income streams through cottage industries can provide additional financial stability and opportunities for your homestead. This chapter explores various cottage industry options that utilize resources from your homestead. You will learn how to identify potential income opportunities, develop cottage industries, and effectively manage your time while maintaining sustainability.

Exploring Additional Income Opportunities

Identify Market Demand: Research and identify niche markets that align with your homestead's resources and capabilities. Consider products such as handmade soaps, herbal products, natural cosmetics, beeswax candles, woodworking crafts, or artisanal food items. Analyze market trends and consumer preferences to ensure there is a demand for your chosen cottage industry.

Assess Resource Availability: Evaluate the resources available on your homestead that can be utilized for cottage industries. For example, if you have an abundance of herbs, flowers, or honey, consider developing herbal teas, essential oils, or honey-based products. Leverage the unique resources and characteristics of your homestead to create a distinct and marketable cottage industry.

Developing Cottage Industries

Research and Skill Development: Gain knowledge and skills related to your chosen cottage industry. Take courses, attend workshops, or learn from experienced individuals in the field. Develop expertise in product formulation, craftsmanship, packaging, and marketing strategies specific to your cottage industry.

Business Planning: Create a detailed business plan that outlines your goals, target market, pricing strategies, marketing tactics, and financial projections. Consider factors such as production costs, supply chain management, distribution channels, and sales strategies.

Product Development and Quality Control: Experiment with product formulations, recipes, or designs to create high-quality and marketable products. Pay attention to details such as ingredient sourcing, product consistency, packaging aesthetics, and labeling compliance.

Balancing Diversification with Sustainability and Effective Time Management

Evaluate Feasibility: Assess the feasibility of incorporating cottage industries into your existing homestead operations. Consider factors such as available time, resources, infrastructure, and the impact on your core homesteading activities. Strive for a balance between diversification and maintaining the sustainability and productivity of your homestead.

Effective Time Management: Prioritize tasks, allocate time blocks, and establish efficient workflows to manage both your core homesteading activities and cottage industries. Develop a schedule that allows for the production, packaging, marketing, and administration of your cottage industry without compromising the well-being of your homestead and yourself.

Collaboration and Delegation: Consider collaborating with family members, neighbors, or hired help to share the workload and responsibilities associated with cottage industries. Delegate tasks that can be handled by others, allowing you to focus on core activities and strategic decision-making.

Start Small and Expand: Begin with a few products or a limited product line to test the market and gain experience. Once you establish a customer base and refine your processes, gradually expand your product offerings based on demand and your capacity to meet it.

Build Brand Identity: Develop a strong brand identity for your cottage industries. Create a compelling brand story, design captivating packaging, and establish a recognizable brand image that resonates with your target market.

Marketing and Promotion: Utilize online platforms, social media, local farmers' markets, craft fairs, or specialty stores to promote and sell your cottage industry products. Leverage the power of storytelling, captivating visuals, and customer testimonials to engage potential customers and build brand loyalty.

Embrace Sustainability: Emphasize sustainable practices in your cottage industries by using organic ingredients, eco-friendly packaging, and ethical production methods. Educate your customers about the environmental and social benefits of supporting sustainable cottage industries.

By exploring additional income opportunities through cottage industries, you can diversify your income streams and maximize the potential of your homestead. Through careful research and skill development, you can identify market demand and develop products that utilize the resources available on your homestead. Balancing diversification with sustainability and effective time management is crucial to ensure the success of your cottage industries without compromising the core activities of your homestead.

Remember to start small and gradually expand your product line as you gain experience and establish a customer base. Building a strong brand identity, implementing effective marketing strategies, and embracing sustainability will help differentiate your cottage industries in the market and attract loyal customers.

Tips and Tricks:

Continual Innovation: Stay updated on industry trends, consumer preferences, and emerging techniques related to your cottage industries. Continually innovate and introduce new products or variations to keep your offerings fresh and exciting for your customers.

Customer Engagement: Foster strong relationships with your customers by engaging with them through social media, newsletters, or events. Encourage feedback, respond to inquiries promptly, and incorporate customer suggestions to enhance your products and services.

Networking and Collaboration: Participate in local farmers' markets, craft fairs, or industry events to network with like-minded individuals and explore collaboration opportunities. Collaborating with other artisans or homesteaders can lead to joint marketing efforts, shared resources, and expanded customer reach.

Stay Compliant: Familiarize yourself with local regulations, permits, and labeling requirements applicable to your cottage industries. Ensure that you comply with food safety standards, product labeling guidelines, and any other legal obligations specific to your products.

Seek Customer Testimonials and Reviews: Encourage satisfied customers to provide testimonials and reviews of your cottage industry products. Display these testimonials on your website or social media platforms to build trust and credibility among potential customers.

By diversifying your income streams with cottage industries, you can leverage the resources of your homestead to create additional revenue streams and increase the financial sustainability of your operation. With careful planning, effective time management, and a focus on quality and customer satisfaction, your cottage industries can become a valuable asset to your overall homesteading business.

Chapter 9: Conclusion - Putting it all together for long-term success

Introduction

Congratulations on reaching the final chapter of this comprehensive guide on how to make money off your homestead. Throughout this book, we have explored a wide range of strategies and opportunities to help you generate income from your homestead. Now, it's time to summarize the key strategies, emphasize the importance of ongoing evaluation and adaptation, and encourage you to pursue your homesteading dreams with confidence.

Summarizing the Key Strategies for Generating Income from Your Homestead

Assessing Your Resources and Setting Goals: Start by evaluating your homestead's assets, including land, climate, and infrastructure. Set clear goals and financial targets to guide your income-generation efforts.

Leveraging Sustainable Agriculture for Profit: Select high-value crops suited to your homestead and implement organic and regenerative farming practices to increase yields and profitability. Explore niche markets and specialty crops to maximize profit margins.

Exploring Alternative Energy Options on Your Homestead: Consider harnessing solar, wind, or hydro power to reduce costs and potentially generate income. Research the feasibility of installing renewable energy systems and explore government incentives and grants available for renewable energy projects.

Creating Value-Added Products from Your Harvest: Discover the benefits of value-added processing and packaging. Learn techniques for preserving, canning, and packaging your harvest to extend shelf life and command higher prices. Develop a product line of jams, jellies, pickles, sauces, or other value-added items.

Tapping into the Agritourism Market: Capitalize on the increasing interest in farm-to-table experiences and agritourism. Create farm tours, workshops, or educational programs for visitors. Explore opportunities for farm stays, on-site lodging, or event hosting.

Maximizing Your Livestock and Poultry Ventures: Identify profitable livestock and poultry breeds for your homestead. Implement efficient animal husbandry practices, feeding strategies, and healthcare protocols. Expand income through meat, dairy, eggs, or fiber production.

Harnessing the Power of Online Marketplaces: Establish a strong online presence through a website, social media, and online marketplaces. Optimize your product listings and descriptions for search engine optimization (SEO). Leverage online platforms to reach a wider audience and increase sales.

Diversifying Income Streams with Cottage Industries: Explore additional income opportunities such as soap making, herbal products, or crafts. Develop cottage industries that utilize resources from your homestead. Maintain a balance between diversification and sustainability, and effectively manage your time.

Emphasizing the Importance of Ongoing Evaluation, Adaptation, and Growth

Generating income from your homestead is an ongoing journey that requires continuous evaluation, adaptation, and growth. Markets change, consumer preferences evolve, and new opportunities arise. Regularly assess the performance of your income-generation strategies, monitor market trends, and seek feedback from your customers. Adapt your offerings, marketing approaches, and business practices accordingly to stay relevant and profitable.

Encouraging Readers to Pursue Their Homesteading Dreams and Achieve Financial Prosperity

Homesteading offers a unique opportunity to live a fulfilling and sustainable lifestyle while generating income. As you conclude this book, we encourage you to pursue your homesteading dreams with passion and determination. Embrace the challenges, learn from your experiences, and celebrate your successes. With careful planning, diligent execution, and a willingness to adapt, you can achieve financial prosperity while living a life connected to nature and self-sufficiency.

Remember, the journey to homestead income is not without its hurdles, but with the knowledge and guidance provided in this book, you are equipped to overcome obstacles and thrive. We wish you all the best in your homesteading endeavors and hope that this book serves as a valuable resource and inspiration

From the Author

Dear Reader,

Thank you for embarking on this homesteading and income-generation journey with me. It has been a privilege to guide you through the process of making money off your homestead and sharing my knowledge and experiences as a fellow homesteader.

Homesteading is more than just a way to generate income; it is a lifestyle choice that brings us closer to nature, fosters self-sufficiency, and allows us to create a harmonious relationship with the land. I hope this book has inspired you to embrace the homesteading lifestyle and discover the many financial opportunities it offers.

Throughout this book, my intention was to provide you with a comprehensive guide that covers various aspects of income generation on your homestead. I aimed to offer practical advice, share valuable insights, and equip you with the tools necessary to succeed in your endeavors.

I encourage you to approach your homesteading journey with passion, dedication, and an open mind. Embrace the challenges and setbacks as opportunities for growth and learning. Be patient with yourself and your progress, knowing that building a successful homestead business takes time, effort, and resilience.

Remember that this book is just the beginning of your homesteading adventure. There is always more to learn, explore, and discover. I encourage you to continue seeking knowledge, connecting with fellow homesteaders, and expanding your skills.

I would love to hear about your experiences, successes, and challenges along the way. Feel free to connect with me through my website or social media platforms, where I share additional resources, tips, and inspiration for the homesteading community.

Lastly, I want to express my gratitude to all the homesteaders, experts, and enthusiasts who have contributed to the knowledge and inspiration behind this book. Your dedication to sustainable living, self-sufficiency, and entrepreneurship is truly commendable, and I am honored to be a part of this community.

May your homestead flourish, your income streams thrive, and your dreams of financial prosperity become a reality. Wishing you abundance, fulfillment, and joy as you continue your homesteading journey.

With warmest regards,

Nicki Lynne xo

Worksheets

Homestead Income Generation Checklist:

Assessing Your Resources and Setting Goals:

- ☐ Evaluate your homestead's assets, including land, climate, and infrastructure.
- ☐ Set clear goals and financial targets for your homestead income.

Leveraging Sustainable Agriculture for Profit:

- ☐ Select high-value crops suited to your homestead.
- ☐ Implement organic and regenerative farming practices.
- ☐ Explore niche markets and specialty crops.

Exploring Alternative Energy Options on Your Homestead:

- ☐ Research and consider harnessing solar, wind, or hydro power.
- ☐ Evaluate the feasibility of installing renewable energy systems.
- ☐ Look into government incentives and grants for renewable energy projects.

Creating Value-Added Products from Your Harvest:

- ☐ Learn techniques for preserving, canning, and packaging your harvest.
- ☐ Develop a product line of value-added items such as jams, jellies, pickles, sauces, etc.

Tapping into the Agritourism Market:

- ☐ Consider farm tours, workshops, or educational programs for visitors.
- ☐ Explore opportunities for farm stays, on-site lodging, or event hosting.

Maximizing Your Livestock and Poultry Ventures:

- ☐ Identify profitable livestock and poultry breeds for your homestead.
- ☐ Implement efficient animal husbandry practices and feeding strategies.
- ☐ Explore meat, dairy, eggs, or fiber production opportunities.

Harnessing the Power of Online Marketplaces:

- ☐ Establish an online presence through a website and social media.
- ☐ Optimize your product listings and descriptions for SEO.
- ☐ Leverage online platforms to reach a wider audience and increase sales.

Diversifying Income Streams with Cottage Industries:

- ☐ Explore additional income opportunities such as soap making, herbal products, crafts, etc.
- ☐ Utilize resources from your homestead to develop cottage industries.
- ☐ Maintain a balance between diversification and effective time management.

Ongoing Evaluation and Adaptation:

- ☐ Regularly evaluate the performance of your income-generation strategies.
- ☐ Stay informed about market trends and consumer preferences.
- ☐ Adapt your offerings and business practices to stay relevant and profitable.

Embracing Sustainability and Community Engagement:

- ☐ Prioritize sustainable practices and responsible land stewardship.
- ☐ Engage with your local community and build strong relationships.

Use this checklist as a reference and mark your progress as you implement each strategy. Remember that building a successful homestead business takes time and perseverance. Celebrate your achievements along the way and continue to learn and grow on your homesteading journey.

Products you should consider selling on your homestead.

- ☐ Fresh fruits and vegetables
- ☐ Herbs and spices
- ☐ Organic eggs
- ☐ Honey and beeswax products
- ☐ Homemade jams, jellies, and preserves
- ☐ Salsa and hot sauces
- ☐ Pickles and fermented vegetables
- ☐ Herbal teas and infusions
- ☐ Culinary herbs and herb blends
- ☐ Artisanal bread and baked goods
- ☐ Fresh and dried flowers
- ☐ Culinary and medicinal mushrooms
- ☐ Goat milk and goat milk products (cheese, yogurt, soap)
- ☐ Fresh herbs and microgreens
- ☐ Homemade sauces and condiments
- ☐ Homemade beauty and skincare products (lotions, balms, soaps)
- ☐ Hand-spun yarn and fiber products
- ☐ Native plants and seeds
- ☐ Potted plants and herb gardens
- ☐ Culinary and medicinal herb plants
- ☐ Firewood and wood products (cutting boards, crafts)
- ☐ Farm-fresh meat (beef, pork, chicken, lamb)

- ☐ Value-added meat products (sausages, jerky, smoked meats)
- ☐ Freshly milled flour and grain products
- ☐ Specialty cheeses and dairy products
- ☐ Handmade crafts and woodworking items
- ☐ Natural dyes and dye kits
- ☐ Freshly pressed juices and cider
- ☐ Herbal remedies and tinctures
- ☐ Homemade pet treats and pet products

Remember to consider the demand and market availability in your area when deciding which products to focus on. Additionally, keep in mind any regulations or certifications that may be required for certain products, such as organic certifications or food handling permits.

Feel free to choose a combination of products that align with your homestead's resources and your target audience's preferences.

Appendix: Resources and Tools

In this appendix, you will find a compilation of useful resources, tools, and additional information to support your journey in making money off your homestead. These resources can provide further guidance, inspiration, and assistance as you explore different income-generating opportunities. Take advantage of the wealth of knowledge available to help you succeed on your homesteading path.

1. Homesteading Organizations and Associations:
    - National Sustainable Agriculture Information Service (ATTRA)
    - Homesteaders of America
    - American Homestead Foundation
    - The Livestock Conservancy
    - Sustainable Agriculture Research and Education (SARE)
2. Online Marketplaces and Platforms:
    - Etsy
    - Shopify
    - Amazon Handmade
    - FarmersWeb

- LocalHarvest
3. Government Resources and Grants:
    - United States Department of Agriculture (USDA)
    - Small Business Administration (SBA)
    - State agricultural departments
    - Rural Development Programs
4. Books and Publications:
    - "The Encyclopedia of Country Living" by Carla Emery
    - "The Market Gardener" by Jean-Martin Fortier
    - "You Can Farm: The Entrepreneur's Guide to Start and Succeed in a Farming Enterprise" by Joel Salatin
    - "The Small-Scale Poultry Flock" by Harvey Ussery
    - "The Profitable Hobby Farm" by Sarah Beth Aubrey
5. Online Resources and Websites:
    - Modern Homesteading Magazine
    - Homesteading Today Forum
    - Permies.com
    - Homestead.org
    - Farm Marketing Solutions

Helpful References

In addition to the resources listed in the appendix, here are some helpful references that can further enhance your knowledge and understanding of the topics covered in this book:

1. Online Courses and Webinars:
    - Udemy: Offers a wide range of online courses on sustainable agriculture, homesteading, and small-scale business management.
    - MOOCs (Massive Open Online Courses): Platforms such as Coursera, edX, and FutureLearn often provide relevant courses on topics like organic farming, permaculture, and sustainable entrepreneurship.
2. Local Extension Offices:
    - Contact your local Cooperative Extension Office or university agricultural department for workshops, seminars, and resources specific to your region.
3. Networking Events and Homesteading Conferences:
    - Attend local farming and homesteading conferences, workshops, and networking events to connect with like-minded individuals

and learn from experienced professionals.
4. Homesteading Blogs and Podcasts:
    - Explore popular homesteading blogs and podcasts, which often share personal experiences, practical tips, and success stories. Some recommended options include "The Modern Homesteading Podcast" and "The Homesteading and Permaculture Podcast."

Remember to stay curious, continue learning, and adapt your strategies based on your unique circumstances and goals. The homesteading community is rich with knowledge, support, and shared experiences. Utilize these resources to expand your expertise and build a thriving and prosperous homestead business.

Please note that the availability and relevance of resources may vary over time, so it's always a good idea to verify the information and seek the most up-to-date resources for your specific needs.

Happy homesteading!